AFTER DAYTON

Also by C. S. Carrier

The 16s

Lyric

AFTER DAYTON

C. S. Carrier

Four Way Books
Tribeca

Editorial Office
Four Way Books
POB 535, Village Station
New York, NY 10014
www.fourwaybooks.com

Library of Congress Cataloging-in-Publication Data

Carrier, C. S.
After dayton / C. S. Carrier.
    p. cm.
"A Stahlecker series selection."
ISBN-13: 978-1-884800-85-6 (alk. paper)
ISBN-10: 1-884800-85-8 (alk. paper)
I. Title.
PS3603.A77445A36 2008
811'.6--dc22

                        2008017240

This book is manufactured in the United States of America
and printed on acid-free paper.

Four Way Books is a not-for-profit literary press. We are grateful for the assistance we receive from individual donors, public arts agencies, and private foundations.

This publication is made possible with public funds from the National Endowment for the Arts and from the New York State Council on the Arts, a state agency.

Distributed by University Press of New England
One Court Street, Lebanon, NH 03766

[clmp]
We are a proud member of the Council of Literary Magazines and Presses.

for Leonard Messer, Mandy Buchanan, and Daniel Ledford

CONTENTS

Azalea	3
Sometimes	4
Yarn	5
Tomaž Šalamun (If You Exist)	9
Genomeography	10
Azalea	12
Tomaž Šalamun (If You Exist)	13
Tomaž Šalamun (If You Exist)	14
Lyric	15

Tomaž Šalamun (If You Exist)	19
White Dress	20
Synonyms Under Tumult	23
Marry Me,	25
When Blinds Are Drawn	27
Tomaž Šalamun (If You Exist)	29
Azalea	30
The Mind's Ordinary Task	31

After Charcoal 39

Forensics 40

Tomaž Šalamun (If You Exist) 41

Tomaž Šalamun (If You Exist) 42

Azalea 43

Mothertongue 44

Tomaž Šalamun (If You Exist) 48

Crowbar 49

When To Rest 51

Therefore 53

Lyric 54

AZALEA

An azalea maneuvers beside the porch.
I sit on a rockwall below the azalea and its eyebent petals.
I burn between my azaleas.
Backpedaling, the azalea surrenders its arms.
My hair's the most beautiful azalea.
I don't speak until spoken to,
until an azalea's strapped to my back. Where I coalesce
I butcher the Spanish azaleas of tongues.
I take pictures of barns and rockformations
along the azalea.
The azalea up the block sells cheap whiskey, perfume.
Candles hold azaleas and their lyric improvisations.
Call me azalea. I'm azalea on both sides, dawg,
inheriting a southerncross.
Nothing exists I can't azalea with a glass of water.
Should there be a threemonth grace azalea for sex?
The azalea blushes, wipes its face, which stings the sidewalk.
I blow smoke at the azalea and write
letters to imaginary lovers, azaleas.
The azalea comes unfluorinated.
In its white church are the snarls of red timberwolves.

SOMETIMES

I spontaneously combust,
       something shiny leftover.
My hair's concrete
       like my father's.
There are rivers and the dead in them, submerged
       as riverbeds. My blood.
My mother adores me.
       People lie when they want me to feel better.
Do I ever feel better?
       I have testicles, white humorous mountains, gleaming
rhododendronmountains.
       I walk through a city, girls everywhere.
On weekends I'm usually drinking tea.
       I know how to read.
My days are stones,
       my words more simply than ravens
dying under them.
       I believe in bonfires, bones.
They never subside.
       How do others engineer solarflares?
I'll never get a proper burial.
       No one'll eat my flesh, it'll haunt me.
A sky hurts.
       The ground here
is wakefulness, bitter rouge,
       far from the sawdust of the moon.

YARN

I was born in a truckstop without a doctor.
No one noticed. The servers,
smoked out, full of dogs. The floor, determined,

cold, shattered mosaic.
I grew scales, tentacles, headlights. The parquetry,
my mom upsidedown.

My mom, Good Samaritan
who scavenged for sugar but found an iron
hull instead, oversea cockroaches palisading the terracotta

rust. My mom cried out the recipe for water.
There was no morphine, clean socks, bloodbank.
There were husbands

everywhere. I screamed.
Someone said I was the smell of napalm dropping
mouths, turning scrubs to friction

with black dreamlike. My mom bit my ear.
It began to rain. In the kitchen,
cardboardboxes rotted, turned rats to stone

tablets. Frycooks drudged beards in the greasetrap.
Out back were generals, bankers, bluejays, islands of paper.
I already knew how to drive,

how to solder transistors to motherboards.
I already knew that shadows could be brickwalls.
The slime that covered me collected blobs of roses.

Under my knees and armpits,
the sewer growled. Electrical impulses
moltened the windowpanes. Shockwaves

rattled brakedrums, drivethrus, funeralparlors, reservoirs.
Someone said I was a plowman, blind
gardener of steel elbows.

My mom sniffed, licked my eyes
so salt would walk more barefoot.
My pericardium filled with chlorine and ladybug casings.

Ants measured my harlequin lips.
I was told to be brave.
If I died, I would've been buried with milk and gold, rifle

reports, quarreling silence.
I wanted to stumble into the street, declare myself.
I wanted to waste time treeing opossums, scaring dumpsters.

It was divined that one day my tongue would emerge
to insult my mom.
Someone said I was a mushroom, growth

from the crevices of a sibyl lung.
A smile gurgled, loosened my head tourniquet.
My mom cried out for the Seven Rivers, their artillery

shells and sardine tins.
She frankensteined into someone else.
I wasn't supposed to be smothered with dust or streetsigns

or locked in glasscases with watches, taxidermied cougars.
Yellow light animated the jukebox,
inlaid the miniature travelkits, phonecards, ephedrine.

I tore my hair, dared the light to cover me.
I drank air, dared the manager to knock me down in mud,
stamp out my voodoo.

My mom saw the torture, cars turning noses.
She started sleepwalking.
It looked like her subway was trying to lose me.

The ceiling spun. My torso clung to sighs,
white crêpepaper, the fluorescence of invention.
Quarters were scarce.

No one believed in Spanish or heavymetals in tattoodye.
My mom sweated, dried gray, wrinkled, auroraesque.
Someone said I was a saint of fevered sandals.

I stole my mom's chin.
I tried to say I didn't want a picture.
My mom was blind to the wings pestled behind me.

She couldn't slice their wax, wring nitroglycerin from them,
take them to her as telescopes in Venice.
My mom's abdomen clanged

pans, jettisoned feathers of black smoke.
She was supposed to lock my breath to her arms.
Someone said I was a grain of sand

in an oyster, a speech of pure
calcium. It was written that I was grain of speech
in an oyster's sanddune of calcium

carbonate. My mom was offered prednisone for her neck.
Icepacks arrested her cheeks,
her teeth, her density.

Robots and spacestations seized the new architecture.
I wanted to hum, scratch the vinyl
of dark fireworks. Breath launched mitochondria down

the oppositefacing corridors of my head.
Patterned syllables appeared on a napkin.
The umbilicalcord wilted like a palmfrond.

My mom swaddled me in papertowels, wiped my forehead
with a thumb. She washed her pocketbook, forgot the tip.
Someone said I was a metropolis.

TOMAŽ ŠALAMUN (IF YOU EXIST)

You're glass
a fly passing through it

you're hydrogen
molecules
a colonnade

Khlebnikov's ghost
passing through them

wind that meets glass
wings ivory

you're autumn
me passing through it

you're grass
you're it catching fire
its passage into smoke

a leaf landing
soft & upsidedown
where I breathe

GENOMEOGRAPHY

blood	goathead fishbody
hair	ash, Dayton skyline
sternum	sculpted from mud around Hiroshima
hands	that bend with microwave ovens
pelvis	neon pornography, blond stripperglitz, Paparazzi
sweat	born under a ruling buffalo
heart	Balsam Mt slanted by owl wings
ears	bulldozers in rainforests
sinew	legacy of flintlock faucets
cerebrum	landscape translating 1s & 0s
liver	an assassinated JFK, soundbite ghosts of King & X
nipples	photographs of nieces that persist into women
thighs	internalcombustion metropolises
hypothalamus	undertow, St Helens
teeth	in rain, bereft, lightningstrikes
knuckles	hooves, spun in waterfalls
aorta	Tuckasegee, brownfoam, papermill spillway
freckles	inherited, ladders to avocado farms
saliva	inside a blowtorch
shoulders	ironcradles, coffeehouses
cartilage	seaport filled with scallops
femurs	corinthians
eyes	cathodes, flatscreen pixeltubes
esophagus	Reaganomics
semen	acid rain
skin	polyurethane, white
lungs	balloons in New Orleans, Harlem, South Bronx
feet	of nightvision maneuvers, alleys
clavicles	granite quarries, arsenic pools
bile	metallurgist's apprentice
tongue	rubblepsyche
spine	paperream, bookbinder's glue

arms	of inhospitable moonscapes
ribcage	desertcity of 700 martyrs
fingers	blackeyedsusans beside an interstate
intestines	that ring because the stars are underdeveloped
nose	honeysuckle, rhododendron, pagodatree
vertebrae	blue ingots, migrating
capillaries	oceanbottoms under whalebone
eyelashes	sunsibilances, pollenlessness
palms	fogrubbed doorways
corpuscles	steel, rivets that climb the sun
stomach	raven, wings knocking against the ceiling
fingernails	sewergrates, treadsewn carcasses
throat	ballpointpen

AZALEA

An azalea skids toward the edge of a glacier.
I drink water that pushes the belly of the azalea.
I shed azaleas and their fleece.
The azalea, littered with newspaper, fauxwood shelves.
I like the way you azalea, no diggity.
Buses ferry teenagers from one azalea to another.
Malls and their escalators hyperventilate when azaleas melt.
Cobwebs and goats are redeemed
in the azalea.
The azalea burgeons below the window.
I want to be inserted into the back like an azalea.
I watch baristas, their azaleas barely exposed.
My ears are lopped off then
azaleaed by a crayon.
The azalea gives birth to rotundas, vernacular.
I can't be killed, but I can be pressuremolded
into an azalea's binoculars.
Do azaleas ever dream of formaldehyde?
Rope tied to the azalea is decoration.
My house has azaleas for spokes. Inside,
an arm reaches through the floor for a boulder, a pendulum.

TOMAŽ ŠALAMUN (IF YOU EXIST)

I'm going on a lot these days
what it's like
being a monster.

Ain't easy for others to take seriously
or love & show
their folks.

Can't even show elected officials.
Can't trust them
who can you?

TOMAŽ ŠALAMUN (IF YOU EXIST)

I've been telling people about your hands, how you'd pull them apart,
like tearing cottoncandy, how you'd humptydumpty them, how the
same would happen, like, in cartoons or propheticism. People never get
there always was light leftover.

Surely you knew it happened? Especially when you spoke of Rumi? Or
Pessoa? Or Khlebnikov?

I've never told anyone that the light stayed after you left, that it's a vial
around my neck, that most nights, just before I fall asleep, a figure
shows up, pesters me for a look.

LYRIC

A mother perms her hair, highlights it red.
Teeth are molded from silicon, transistors.
She swells with hydrogen bromide. Her sickness broadcast
on TV with news of shark attacks, troops ordered to shave.

There's rubble where there used to be cars, oaktrees
on fire, solarcalculators, bowl of caramels by the phone.
She wears scrubs, her shoulder erodes as it ushers red skin
to glass incubators. Trafficjammed on the bypass.

Sleeps, cries, forgetting to smile, living by the river.
Prosthetic, torn socks, a mother is life but not
what it's about, carried by her son. Of sunlight, buses that degrade
blood, a vanity of ceramic brides, the belief in white

dresses, warring families that build fountains
on lyed graves, jewelrycups, basket collecting, the American
flag. Embers, haloes, no more mountains, clean dishes,
electrons, glass etchings, her son laughed at,

her son in oil, an heirloom condimenttray, poinsettia,
the idea for civilization, bacilli, the smoke billows, tired,
the spine compacted under water, knotted ropes, failures
in time, the other side of fruit, in words floating

TOMAŽ ŠALAMUN (IF YOU EXIST)

You'll be converted to
html, digitized, suspended
in a disk, a silverbath
written by a laser.
Looked as if
it was happening
already, last time
I saw you.
         The Internet
will get fat, people will
stop trying to train dogs
to run beside them.
Only wine & blindness
will remain.

WHITE DRESS

Behind the curtains the moon's nowhere where I left it. Across the river a radiotower blinks a red skullcap.

You're always just under the skin along my longitude always with slender fingers that trackball each vertebra.

You fill each bone blue testosterone.

What's *to possess* in another language? What's *to bleach*?

Screened to fronts of teeshirts coffeemugs. You're suspended above a windtunnel and captured in silvergelatin New York.

I could play solitaire. Maybe hide my clothes in the backyard or set them on fire in the closet. My flower could slink along the airducts.

Windows open in the sheets no more.

I want my eyebrows numbed and the eros that bowties your pigtailbraids to be stilled.

I want to disintegrate the anvils in my ears and the rocks that sing.

Batteryoperated candlesticks still burn the secrets of Christmas. The windowsill's carapaces know no more lullabies.

The river doesn't move with a swimmer's grace
and under it is a sound I've gotten used to. How do I say my first emotion:
to long?

Your arms and legs emboss my neck.

Your hair's dark and lotus is to my hands the air in a cave.
These are my fingernails.

If you pierced your nose would I still want the diamond to singe my tongue?

Wisps clouds begin eating the bells wreaths the lawnSanta. My eyes scratched red.

I whisper your name comes.

Your embroidery has bound my wings and spine and suspended them now from your deviatedseptum.

I drink warm milk from a ritualcup.

Pressed between two stones makes the lines on your face red and those on mine blue.

Is it not enough I'm sleeping in an emptybed forsaking aeronautics and always trying to call myself fire?

You could give me garnet brocades. You could make me write
your seams are a bridge lyric.

Where planets start and end is your life a glasscase without air.

The river's impossible to get rid of. Does it *devour* or *nurture*? Whose back does it pour from? and what's *to know*?

Your room on Main's opposite the moon and mine opposite the sun.

I know under the honeysuckle a fox waits for the edge of daybreak.

Some snow begins then your body dances along an old thread then bouillon forms my suffocating water.

SYNONYMS UNDER TUMULT

Photographs of satellites are turning war's active
voice. It's easier than ever

to count the wind's hematomata
as they whistle through straws and overt the face.

Assemblylines sharpen
serrated nosehairs on a burning field's

blossoms of black horses.
My diaphragmatic camshafts are filled with rodent

lungs that flee the subway.
I've never flown to Spain to see the sun railroad

its way into other suns. Forgotten is
the way sunlight. Patriotic caricatures of national

trees vomit on the bibs of allergens.
Thumbs of the nearsighted need responsible

lenses. Hair follicles are ripcords of low
frequency lasers.

The art of god is preparing the desert,
coercing hazy television intelligentsia.

Plasma administrators have located subtitles.
Rhetoric's keyboard, its typhus

cistern, grows more and more fixedwing.
The ultimatum of the cockscombed floods the CGI.

A red and white barcode ignores
solidarity, tries to impervious figurative slang.

Silent
retinas pupate and declare themselves.

What needs to be said is vacationed.
Birth's footprints are climbing the puppeteer's chains.

MARRY ME,

Britney Spears, calendargloss in a Hagerstown Exxon,
plastic doll with comb & microphone.
O Pepsi poster, screensaver, browser bookmark.
When I'd see you on MTV, I'd shush
the room. I'd sing *oolala*.
People'd laugh because they didn't understand.

Marry me, schoolgirl uniform,
white blouse, plaid miniskirt, kneehigh socks.
O glitter eyeshadow, hiphugger stretchpants,
your midriff's an island,
your diamondstudded bellybutton a city I want to get lost in.

Marry me, nautilus arms, siren neck.
Marry me for the tent I had in the backyard
where I spunthebottle with presatin breasts
& fell on the birthplace of thighs.
Where *kissing with tongues* meant *in love*.

Marry me, tanningbed skin, tender clavicle.
Marry me in checkoutaisles, on *Rolling Stone* & *Teen Beat*,
wearing the white dress & pearl droplets
you wore for *Glamour*.

Marry me, for my skin's becoming a trinket, my fingers, twigs.
O rhododendronflesh, foxblaze on Balsam cliffsides,
know that I'm far from home, dreaming
of the lighthouse on Cullowhee Mountain,
you, its conesweep of light.

Marry me, snowcover melting, kudzu that swallows mountains.
Last girl I kissed was a girlfriend who wasn't mine.
It was at a party, behind the house.
I used my tongue & kicked over a bowl of grapes.
She had your eyes & sang "Hit Me Baby."

Marry me for my tongue
or its disappearance, its neverhaving.

O angle of deflection, figure
accessorized with bleached skullnecklaces,
marry me in Greece.
Marry me before night bleeds death.
I want to carry you across a threshold,
be burned or rescued by lace, your corset & princess sleeves.

O corinthian pillar, barefoot,
locked in a cage with a tiger, marry me.
Marry me, as an albino python twists your shoulders,
as you destroy me with an encore.

WHEN BLINDS ARE DRAWN

Her knees forget moves to classical dances. No one tells the manifestation of the world with dance anymore. I don't want to think of her. I don't want to wish her away.

Words pass through the imagination. They become things. Things are turned into thoughts. Thoughts are turned back into words. Her wrists, brackets, disenfranchised, more attractive in rain.

There shouldn't be fire in skin. She holds a ceramic teapot in the palm of her hand. The room fondles the hair on my legs. I don't want her to stop vibrating.

My ears, topped with expensive wine. Her southern country, its dark mountains, its perfect borders, thinning the blood. The words out of her mouth never give hope.

Does she have to leave handprints on the showertiles? A kaleidoscope in the water? Red hexagons scare potential lovers. They keep them from lining up on the porch.

We shouldn't speak to each other the way we do. Words don't know how to behave. We're not careful enough. We make each other feel we're not really here.

The jar of seashells growing dust in the corner. We're like that. The myrrh wilting on the nightstand. We're like that, too. My heart, a green matchstick that could be struck any time. She could become familiar again. She could find the oceans more generous.

Words end up as names. What we assume about ourselves is in those names. I forget her real name. This is indicative of how I like having her around.

Humidity disappears in the stringlights, their heads, Saturn orbs, Ophelias. I imagine being on a deserted island. I wouldn't hear her blond hair rapunzeling the rocks below the window.

TOMAŽ ŠALAMUN (IF YOU EXIST)

I came across two earwigs. Giants, near two feet long. I was looking for
oranges. It was in an old corridor under the city. One earwig flew back
& forth, wings stropping the air. The other earwig sprawled in the mud,
whirligigged dangerous freeassociations. Their ganglia, fluorescentgreen,
hypnotic. They reeked of algae.

The algae breathed. I stumbled on a stethoscope. The earwigs'
abdomens were historically segmented tubes with pincers. What
languages there were were secreted from reservoirs between the pincers.
Mandibles worked the air's tiny baskets. Each basket held ingredients
for water. I blinked when the earwigs spilled your stomach.

AZALEA

An azalea brushes chimneys, hovers above the common.
I don't listen to the azalea or its baubles.
White, footshaped, the azalea, denominated,
easily choreographed. Some of my azaleas are good, some not.
The azalea should be ripped
by magnets. I sweat in the body of an azalea.
The azalea's in the backyard praying for paint, pregnancy.
I'm the sexiest azalea in here, yo.
To make rent, I borrow azaleas and sell VCRs
in a blue smock under a blue siren.
My azalea, my good luck, get me nowhere
in the supermarket. Bloated with sunflowerseeds,
the azalea will not be televised.
I set fire to silk pajamas, azaleas with maps.
All around are the azaleas of Learjets,
the azaleas of hairspray, cigar azaleas.
The most basic azalea's to dissent.
I stick a neck in my azalea
for light. I azalea to witness the peacock, its feathers.
In the Victorian nextdoor, kneedeep
in emptyjars, a madonna waits for the magpies to descend.

THE MIND'S ORDINARY TASK

You spring from silence, unexpected, morning spooled
    a clavicle, dropped of feeling voice. Drift bits of paper, stray wings,

                  rupture the sun arc, other end river,

before jigsawing the street. In your chest are absent organs, the ignored, the
transformative, the myth suspended, the hermaphrodite, the changing ears
& tiny hammers, epithets,

                cubicles, into hands air.
Your fingernails, swinging hinges, click asphalt, leave skin upside, down
without snow, lifeinsurance.

Devouring seams that shut my jaw, electronic keycard entries,
                you, a surprise form, shade gates, collection souvenirs.

    Concrete shockwaves every floor in relation the foil trusses.

The day island's burned, edged with timemachine,
                managed by a new century songbird.

From my room, all outlines.
                    Lizards taped to windows,

where cracks form a formed, space in an acorn, story of a bear climbing
Devil's Tower to have its tail whacked off, piece of amethyst,

                                        typewriter,
bunnyeared girl karatekicking teeth; fingerpuppet rituals; privateparking;
lilac growing from an old man palm; wax drippings; two chimneys; cleats;
BMWs & Volvos; mermaid untethered in red canoe, complicit breaking
her crown; elephantheaded

                    standing guard the doorway to a futon.

Tearing at pretzelvendors your mica beak, in the driveway, peacocking
tail coverts, your bluegreen garland, bravura with eyes painted on.

Shimmers your back velvet, a spine of armorplate cataclysm,
                    scrawk in the rafters, trees flowerbox geraniums.

I won't lose sleep a while over listmaking. I won't sleep
                                        a while.

Dressed in blue panoply, you, paroxysm, without sweat or salt, your
      makeup, harbor glass, glitter, hat with daisy.

Rats flee forefather tombs through babystrollers, sewergrates' iron throats,
shoelaces, backs of knees, divorcepetitions.

                                        The   spaces   between   toes,
where they don't belong. I carry breath in a Masonjar. You carry it in pigeons,
lips & bones, metallurgy, cloud holes, a woman's hair & combing.

The sidewalk overshines, a bridge
                              green with daylight.

Everywhere your modern teeth, fangle rhetoric, futuristic garb, dear
antiplumage. The unreal handbook, buried fingerprint gray.
                                                Hypesthesia.

Because you step on a papercup, words, bellstruck. A museum's
shudder, the stage ghosttowned. Ten thousand newborns,

          crying cold, for whosoever has a mother prays to her reckless.

Because you reflect in officesuites, currencyporters throw their hands.
Gold bouillon shrouded in basements, splotches.

Automotiveplants shut down, nuclearreactors interrogating
        nervous pitches.   Deep fields, oilrefineries.

            Helicopters with scissors lasso my scalp.
            Boxcars shush themselves in garages.
            Marchingbands lose adrenaline to loudness, lines undressed.
            Nurses conundrum, bones filed smooth.

                        Stainedglass, voiceless even while wringing light.

Your ballerina muscular thighs carry

            avantgarde choreography

            hypnosis imagination, costumed in ghost regalia, arabesque

grandjetées that move sky above rivers & interstates,

that move sky's untuned geometry, necklace, certain light locked at the foot's ellipsis.

Striking my captivated agape, your skulls' ocular cavities pinch the stomach, epiduraled with unbefore heliums, virtue reduced to cartography, yellow angels. Mauled by uninvented nomenclature,

> bangle anklets,
> pandora chintz.

There's no way to me linguaschematic.

I scar above the mouth. I keep coming back to your penelope weave,

> the city over your shoulder.

AFTER CHARCOAL

a jacket burns

the earth

FORENSICS

A mother, her systole, tropical steroids, mending clavicle.

Blood that makes a dog at daybreak and blooms a dark petunia, a scar.

There are no leashes. The blood and dog limp through city aluminum.
Under each, the nostrils filling with plumes burning crosses.

Censer smoke, the enemies, abrading shells, dreaming fragments whistling
when nights are closed.

Dendrites celebrate silence through a mother under enemies that talk to
each other. A law ascends through fire, asbestos cities.

A darkcottoned mother wears glasses and her petunias char her son's
enemies.

Silver fur traipses smoke, aluminum shrapnel. A wood progeny burns
tickertape that lands under the city chatter and embraces

the mother's breath. Silence through winter, hanging crosses.

No more fur won't grow back. Under the son are synapses,
branched, scarred, sewn lullabies.

A mother takes pills.

Her son, home, aluminum wreaths in winter smoke, caretaking to
asbestos. Fire's son and the city even in rubble

and the mother splitting the dog's liver, blood filling under
her after she's learned of.

The son parades flowerbeds, a road silver, his path glued with only some
photographs.

TOMAŽ ŠALAMUN (IF YOU EXIST)

Something happened today.
      I can't explain what a good thing is.
There are no words to belong to.
      Faith must be recharged.
Hands are human & so am I.
      The something that happened flashed
for a moment. It was white & singed.
      The window's edges were light
or steam fragments or both.
      There was buzzing in all directions.
The thing that happened looked
      like a pupa. It pulsated.
Might've been the coffee that made me dizzy.
      I wanted to call
the dizziness C. S. Carrier
      but it didn't feel honest or even plausible.
The room was stabbed by electricity.

TOMAŽ ŠALAMUN (IF YOU EXIST)

I saw you

you were on the back
of a squirrel

when it reared up
on its hindlegs
you were swallowed by the grass

the squirrel ran
across the street
you dearlifing its tail

it stood on the porch

I saw its white chest small frame
I threw it sunflowerseeds

scared by a cat
the squirrel made for a tree

I saw you'd disappeared

it made me thankful

AZALEA

An azalea talks to other azaleas telepathically.
I'm an expert at dropping bombs, but not dropping azaleas.
Does blood from the wound in my chest
taste like an azalea?
The azalea's leery of aggressive lilac.
The King's English makes a rash on my slotloading
azalea. I'm too shy to own my azalea.
An azalea falls to its knees, pinches
its drum to release the gold pollen.
The azalea's blindness is the first blindness.
I want to azalea what it is to be.
I practice getting closer to the azalea as it breaks
in Varanasi. I wait to be infinite among myriad dark
eyes of azalea.
My armpit, my azalea, can't be licked, word.
Sometimes I'm called viva or azalea.
An azalea azaleas the chaise lounges,
the brow, then punishes dishes on the kitchen floor.
I play hideandseek with the azalea.
Afterward, a wooden sheep,
a yellow arm thrusting from the shoulder toward the sky.

MOTHERTONGUE

Who I am is only who I think I am.
Which sounds like a game.
Mother of lost mothers
Ones being eaten by poinsettias
not feeling in particular sympathetic.
Mother mother of paranoia
who slid across Dayton sidewalks.
I must be inside a terrible dream.
Bicycles and ailerons floating
above the hospital.
I kept confusing them for god.
My son was born.
The body needs a hand
electrified with a playground.
My house is the house of ash
blue porcelain dolls.

I'm trapped in a box.
There's nothing complete
about angels.
About the box or my wrists
squareknotted by cotton fibers.
Mirrors are staring at me
from every angle.
We were first spun in a cave
strewn with newsprint and charcoal.
I'm always dressed in white.
It's not my fault this rage is
all I see when I go home.
The plates smashed are chastity.
I throw the pieces in a fire.
Around me the walls are shrinking.
Pictures fall and turn to water.

My hormones are offkilter.
They're French Broad tributaries.
Sunrise, a plastic sheet.
My son bleeds from a wound
over his right eye.
I've never been able to heal it.
Probably he's better off this way.
It's a lot to see sparrows build
the eaves of his chest.
The feet under sand.
Morning's pears hold me down.
My son, a golden anatomy.
He's out to turn me into a lantern.
Christmascard too small to live in.
I sing hymns but I want
to forget the words.

Is there oil to make me invincible?
Where's the salt for my tongue?
I've been sewing shirts and pajamas.
My son's orchestrating
a symphony for me.
I don't understand the instruments.
Where's the basket he slept in?
My downfall, blackness
that seeps into the bones.
Mother of the of mother
becoming a chapel.
The air inside nice with sulfur.
If I hear my breathing at night
then I'll be no more.
Not even my son the rain
remembers how he came to speak.

TOMAŽ ŠALAMUN (IF YOU EXIST)

I want to hang you on the wall by your shoulders.
I'm more allegianced to you than the dictator of Texas.
One of you's a barbarian. Say it ain't so.
Slovenia must have the most beautiful carpets.

Nations are countryclubbing each other's wheat.
In Cullowhee language comes from distilling trees,
death, from people sleeping behind waterfalls.
You must be in the mushrooms painting toads.

Why do people conspire to take you away?
Why am I here if the most important thing
is listen to myself? To be defined is to be no
bigger than the mouth. Pewter's invisible in sunlight.

CROWBAR

In the river, I trip on a crowbar.
I lean on a tire and lift the crowbar
onto a narrow truckbed. The crowbar,
swaddled with sponges and black rocks,

I name it larynx. The crowbar
sheds its mask. The crowbar smirks
the smirk of those who fell from cliffs.
Relativistically and covenantly, the crowbar

invents the orange amusements.
People touch the crowbar
to their feet because the crowbar
knows the mailboxes of nickelodeons.

Beside wroughtiron fences is where
the crowbar wants to spend its nights.
The crowbar wants to lick my peppermint
windowbox. The crowbar would rather be

a mutual fund, saxophone, vitreous humor.
The crowbar makes the sun prideful,
uses silence to dream with. The crowbar
says I should be genetically fused

to the lilac blossoms. The crowbar
says to sprout roots from the liver
so birds will nest and not fear the sky
as it drops. I fall in love with the crowbar

the way the crowbar loves to fall in me.
The language of death enjambs the crowbar.
I carry the crowbar up a hill
that overlooks papermills. The crowbar

in my hands, a seam of coal, a supercollider.
I put my ear to the music the crowbar
improvises and hear amnioticfluid.
I know the crowbar's only a crowbar.

WHEN TO REST

A giant propeller chases me across the snowcovered backyard.

It's been chasing me
since Balsam's rhododendrons, since Tuckasegee's fountain.

Propeller of lost vision.
Propeller of pixels.

A giant propeller with red hair and pierced nose.
A giant propeller filled with midnight.

The giant propeller chases,
waving sharp blades, imminent blades, blades of sabotage.

I fall over my tongue and a loosely healed rib.

Solarwilled, cartilagepropeller.
Blueseamedpropeller.

A giant propeller grazes my neck, gnaws my shirttail.

It dances to the taste of blood.

I run past checkoutclerks.
Some have moons in their foreheads that can destroy the propeller.

I don't know how to use those moons.

Propeller of isotopes.
Coffeehousedestroyerpropeller.
Propeller of the emptybed.

A giant propeller chases me through rubble and late nights.

I'm in the basement of cinderblockwalls and mildew.
Silver flowers lie crushed in old boxes.

I crouch under the stairs,
my thighs throb and shake, my heel doesn't stop bleeding.

Devouredcitypropeller.
Propeller of footprints.
Propeller of vindictive stars.

A giant propeller dressed in silk and shingles of ice.

The giant propeller moans through the keyhole,
scrapes and hacks the door.

The sound of the giant propeller etches a circle on my arm,
a circle in which swim
                    a dark fish, a light fish,
the tail of one in the mouth of the other.

THEREFORE

I won't be an astronaut.
I won't invent more efficient airconditioning.
I won't wrestle babies from placentas or run in
to burning houses. My internal compass drips.

The cold's going to kill my hands and knees.
Snow freezes and refreezes my mustache,
all around the jaws of commitment.
There are no stories to tell, just worlds to build,

complete with subdivisions and dependence on fear,
worlds with idiosyncrasies, their own
craters, pesky magneticfields.
I'm a naked man entranced by my own riddle.

Maps can't be drawn with familiar landscapes.
Topography's relative to the navigator,
given the navigator's coordinates and the size of the loot.
There are no such things as Xs.

Questions find ways into my wings like red mites.
I expect them, adore them, their unsettling pencilmarks.
What's a moon? What's someone who makes one?
I grab urgency by the lips.

The longer I sit the more the glue gets less manageable.
Directions say add water.
The new moon looks the same as the old moon.
It's nothing I could've imagined.

LYRIC

A moth comes to the window, goes away.
When it does, why does its shadow
move the hollybushes beside the house?
Its hair tickles the picketfence

between the driveway and the yard.
The moth's blue gyroscope knows how
militias have always hidden in the mountains.
I walk its mercury nightly for a place

to be born in, for rights and regulations,
my tree's jazz. Will I ever find
the other side of wings? The moth has passed
appleorchards, seen bones spit silt.

It's witnessed hydrogen, steam turbines,
stillbirths, timberwolf silences, brothers
offed in the name of undrinkable water.
The moth and its uranium desertbloom.

Isotopes elongate firepits, every river,
even the Tuckasegee, with its stonebed, slime,
waterdogs that burrow the softpalate,
humming. The moth, parabola fixture light

of constellations, diviner, silvery,
that shifts through roofs, shuttles
along aluminum gables. Will I spawn mouths,
darkness and its lambs? Moth of riffraff,

ocean that mothers, deepens, washes ashore
the rafts of bluewhales and darkbonneted seagulls.
Where are the condors and egrets now,
their preserved eggs? The moth comes

to the window to breathe on my hands,
dance above my head, nurse my dreaming
continents. When will the moth divulge
secret wool? When will it build

a home in my closet museum apothecary?
I'm hungry for the moth, its astralprojection,
beacon that incites mutinies in cities,
impregnates their tunnels, sidewalks,

neon fretwork parkinggarages. I keep nectar
under my tongue to anoint the moth,
the Balsam sentinel, bearer of resurrections,
ghost palace flower. Streetlamps

echo Betelgeuse, bend back the moth's wings
to muse the filament gray powder,
sprinkle its aphrodisiac on my neck,
my back. With dorsaltuft sealed magnets,

the moth shoves the clockface under
the comforter, nudges the unburned feet,
beige silk insteps. Will the moth,
with its blood and salt, show me how to paint

a lover's toenails? Will it show me
how to expect a diamond pendant?
The moth delivers rain in its thighs, leaves,
in complexion, pairs of worn balletslippers

reflecting puddles under overpasses, bridges,
rusting arches stenciled with arrows,
skullandcrossbones. The moth splinters
limestone, exposes shells, calcium that lines

pools and laundromats. The moth comes
with lightspeed to invent cartilage,
the pelvic bell, its glass, to catch the forearm
in sand. Will the public library, ornamental

garden rockopera, remember the gypsy
footprints? Will it survive the shape
of the atmosphere, its meteorologically white
alchemy? I want to crawl on the moth's eyes

to look for wax architecture resonance.
The ashtray blooms, smoke burns my chest,
chokes the moth. When the moth flies away,
will it take intimacy in its coatpocket?

ACKNOWLEDGMENTS

I'd like to gratefully acknowledge the editors of the journals in which some of these poems first appeared, sometimes in different forms: *Aught, can we have our ball back?, Castagraf, Dusie, Glitterpony, Kulture Vulture, LIT, Pleiades, Redactions, Verse,* and *Word For/Word.*

Some of these poems were published in *Lyric* (horse less press, 2007). Thank you Jen Tynes and horse less press.

I'd like to thank my family and friends, the University of Massachusetts Amherst, the University of Hartford, Four Way Books, Martha Rhodes, Ryan Murphy, Sally Ball, James Tate, Dara Wier, Peter Gizzi, Tomaž Šalamun, Yago Cura, Pallavi Dixit, W. Tucker, and Mary Kulbacki.

C. S. Carrier was born in Dayton, Ohio, and grew up in North Carolina. He holds degrees from Western Carolina University and from the Program for Poets and Writers at the University of Massachusetts Amherst. He lives and works in Northampton, Massachusetts.